This book
belongs to

_____

God Loves Me

Bible Promises for Little Hearts

Written and Illustrated by
Kathy Arbuckle

BARBOUR
PUBLISHING, INC.

© MCMXCVII by Barbour Publishing, Inc.

ISBN 1-57748-236-0

All scripture quotations are taken from the Authorized
King James Version of the Bible.

Published by Barbour Publishing, Inc.
          P.O. Box 719
          Uhrichsville, Ohio 44683
          http://www.barbourbooks.com

 Member of the
Evangelical Christian
Publishers Association

Printed in China

Contents

I Love My Family–*parents' duties* 6

I Am Happy–*contentment, joy,*

      obedience, praise *10*

I Am Strong–*courage* *18*

I Have Jobs–*laziness* *22*

I Tell the Truth–*honesty* *24*

I Get Mad–*anger* *28*

I Am Scared–*fear, peace, protection,*

      enemies, help *30*

I Am Sorry–*forgiveness, repentance* *36*

I Really Am Rich–*money, sharing* *44*

God Loves Me

Children, obey your parents in all things: for this is well pleasing unto the Lord.

COLOSSIANS 3:20

Do your parents tell you to do things?

Your mommy and daddy love you very much. They always want what is best for you. That's why they tell you what to do. Did you know that God put you and your parents together? God wants you to do what Mommy and Daddy say to do. God always knows what is best for you.

God Loves Me

Train up a child in the way he should go: and when he is old, he will not depart from it.

PROVERBS 22:6

Do your parents talk to you about God?

Your mommy and daddy want you to know about God. They want you to know how much God loves you. Someday you and your parents will live together with God in heaven.

God Loves Me

But godliness with contentment is great gain.

I TIMOTHY 6:6

Do you have everything you want?

What you want and what you need are two different things. You may want lots of toys that you don't have. But God knows what you need. God has given you family, friends, sunshine and rain, food, clothes, and especially love. That's all you really need to be happy.

God Loves Me

My lips shall greatly rejoice when I sing unto Thee.

PSALM 71:23

Do you like to sing?

We can tell God how happy He makes us by singing happy songs to Him. He loves to hear you sing. Your songs show God how much you love Him.

God Loves Me

And thou shalt do that which is right and good in the sight of the Lord: that it may be well with thee. DEUTERONOMY 6:18

Do you think about God?

In the Bible, God's special Book, God tells how He wants you to live. When you live as God wants, you will be happy. When you live as God wants, God will show you how happy He is. He will always take care of you.

God Loves Me

I will bless the Lord at all times: His praise shall continually be in my mouth.

PSALM 34:1

What has God given you today?

You have so many reasons to say thank you to God. Just think... God gives you a night of sleep and a day of sunshine. He gives you a friend to laugh with, a dog to hug, and a mommy or daddy to listen. Thank God every day for all He has given you. God wants you to be happy!

18 *God Loves Me*

Be of good courage, and He shall strengthen your heart, all ye that hope in the Lord.

PSALM 31:24

Can God make you strong?

God made the whole universe and everything that is in it. God knows everything, too. If you love God, God will make you strong and brave.

God Loves Me

The Lord is my helper, and I will not fear what man shall do unto me.

HEBREWS 13:6

Do you know someone who picks on you?

Almost everybody has known a bully. God says that we should love bullies. We should even pray for them! Ask God to help you. With God as your helper, you can face anyone and not be afraid.

God Loves Me

He that tilleth his land shall have plenty of bread.

PROVERBS 28:19

Do you have jobs to do at home?

Do you have to make your bed or put your toys away? Everyone has jobs to do. God says that if we do our jobs, we will make our families happy. God is happy when He sees you helping your parents and others.

God Loves Me

Ye shall not steal, neither deal falsely, neither lie one to another.

LEVITICUS 19:11

Have you ever told a lie?

Even though you don't want to get in trouble, telling a lie is a bad idea. God's Son Jesus said He is the way, the truth, and the life. Like Jesus, you should always tell the truth.

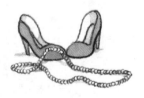

God Loves Me

Lying lips are abomination to the Lord, but they that deal truly are His delight.

PROVERBS 12:22

Do lies make God happy?

The Bible says God hates lies. When you tell a lie you hurt yourself and others. God knows when you lie and when you tell the truth. The truth makes God happy.

God Loves Me

A soft answer turneth away wrath: but grievous words stir up anger.

PROVERBS 15:1

Do you get mad sometimes?

Sometimes someone or something can make you very mad. God wants you to be like His Son, Jesus. Jesus said you should be nice to each other. You should use kind words.

God Loves Me

For I the Lord thy God will hold thy right hand, saying unto thee, Fear not; I will help thee.

ISAIAH 41:13

Why does your daddy or mommy hold your hand when you cross the street?

Your parents want to keep you safe. Sometimes things around you can be scary. God knows this, too. He doesn't want you to be afraid. God is with you-- and your daddy and mommy-- to help you be careful.

God Loves Me

And the peace of God, which passeth all understanding, shall keep your hearts and minds through Christ Jesus.

PHILIPPIANS 4:7

Do you ever wonder what will happen next?

Maybe you feel scared when you see pictures of wars. Or maybe someone you love is sick and you wonder if they'll ever get better. God is in control of the whole world. In fact, the whole universe! Can you imagine how big God is? God is able to take away every scary thought. God is able to do anything.

God Loves Me

I will both lay me down in peace, and sleep: for Thou, Lord, only makest me dwell in safety.

PSALM 4:8

Are you ever afraid of the dark?

Many people are scared of things they can't see. But God is with you all the time. Every single minute and second of the day and night God is there. Wherever you go, you are not alone. You don't have to be scared of the dark anymore.

God Loves Me

The Lord is gracious, and full of compassion; slow to anger, and of great mercy.

PSALM 145:8

How do you feel when you do something bad?

God loves you very much. But He feels sad when He sees you do something bad. Tell Him how sorry you are. Ask Him to help you do the right thing next time.

God Loves Me

And be ye kind one to another, tenderhearted, forgiving one another, even as God for Christ's sake hath forgiven you.

EPHESIANS 4:32

What does it mean <u>to forgive</u>?

If someone does something bad to you, and they say they are sorry, you <u>forgive</u> them if you say, "That's okay." Jesus said you should forgive others seventy times seven. (Let's see. That would be 490 times.) That is a lot of forgiving, but that is what God wants you to do.

God Loves Me

If we confess our sins, He is faithful and just to forgive us our sins.

I JOHN 1:9

How does God forgive you?

The second you tell God you are sorry, God forgives you. God says, "That's okay." You should also tell God that you will try very hard never to do that bad thing again. God is your Heavenly Father. He wants you to learn from your mistakes.

God Loves Me

He that covereth his sins shall not prosper: but whoso confesseth and forsaketh them shall have mercy.

PROVERBS 28:13

When you do something wrong, do you try to pretend you haven't?

God always knows the truth. He sees everything you do. Don't blame someone else for your actions or tell a lie. Tell God you are sorry. God will forgive you.

God Loves Me

A little that a righteous man hath is better than the riches of many wicked.

PSALM 37:16

Will lots of money make you happy?

Only for a little while. No matter how much money you have, you will never have enough to buy everything you want. And if money is all you want, you won't be happy. Only God can give you real happiness. You are really rich if you know God loves you and you love God.

God Loves Me

Inasmuch as ye have done it unto one of the least of these my brethren, ye have done it unto Me.

MATTHEW 25:40

Do you like to give presents ?

You don't have to be rich to give a present to someone. Sharing whatever you might have can make someone happy. You could give a present of your time or something special you made all by yourself. You could give a toy you don't play with anymore. Whenever you share with others, you are sharing with Jesus.

And He took them up in His arms, put His hands upon them, and blessed them.

MARK 10:16